Introduction to Baking

No-Knead Bread in Bread Pans

(Plus... Guide to Bread Pans)

Updated to Include New "Hands-Free Technique"
and "Poor Man's Dutch Oven"

From the kitchen of
Artisan Bread with Steve

Updated 7.30.2018

By
Steve Gamelin

Copyright © 2014 by Steve Gamelin

All rights reserved. No part of this book may be used or reproduced, stored in a retrieval system, or transmitted in an form or by an means—electronics, mechanical, or any other—except for brief quotations in print reviews without prior permission of the author.

Now that I have met the standard legal requirements I would like to give my personal exceptions. I understand this is a cookbook and anyone who purchases this book can, (a) print and share the recipes with their friends, as you do with your other cookbooks (of course, it is my hope they too will start to make no-knead bread and buy my cookbooks) and (b) you may share a recipe or two on your website, etc. as long as you note the source and provide instructions on how your audience can acquire this book.
Thanks – Steve

Table of Contents

Note from Steve 2

Overview 3

Ingredients 4

    Flour 4

    Salt 5

    Yeast 5

    Water 6

    Flavor Ingredients 6

Technique & Tips 7

    Prep..7

    Combining Ingredients...7

    1st Proofing (bulk fermentation) 7

    Degas, Pull & Stretch 9

    Roll-to-Coat...9

    Garnish & Baste 9

    Divide & Shape..9

    2nd Proofing 10

    Score 10

    Bake 10

    Storing Bread & Dough 11

    Equipment & Bakeware 11

Guide to Bread Pans 14

    Basic Loaf Sizes 14

Basic Pan Sizes 14

Types of Bread Pans...15

    Standard Loaf Pans 16

    Cast Iron..18

    Stoneware, Glass, Etc...19

"Traditional" No-Knead Bread... proofs 8 to 12 hours.............................21

    Country White Bread (First "traditional" loaf)................................22

    Cheddar Cheese Bread (bread pan)..24

    Multigrain Country White Bread (bread pan)...................................26

    Honey Whole Wheat Bread (bread pan) 28

No-Knead "Turbo" Bread... ready to bake in 2-1/2 hours........................30

    Country White "Turbo" Bread (First "Turbo" loaf) 32

    Country White Bread (bread pan... garnished with sesame seeds).................34

    Multigrain Country White Bread (bread pan... garnished with oats) 36

    Congratulations... You're a Master Baker!..38

Additional Recipes 39

    Beer Bread (bread pan) 40

    Honey Oatmeal Bread (bread pan | garnish) 42

    Harvest 8 Grain Whole Wheat Bread (bread pan)............................44

    Deli Rye Bread (bread pan) 46

    Mediterranean Olive Bread (long loaf pans | half loaves | baste) 48

    Cinnamon Raisin Bread (small bread pan)..50

    Italian Sesame Sandwich Bread (poor man's Dutch oven) 52

    Garlic Bread (poor man's Dutch oven | long loaf pans) 54

Author's Note

When you look at a recipe,
think of it as sheet music.
It's the instrument and voice that transforms
sheet music into a song and gives it individuality.

Recipes are written for general use
waiting for the right instrument (bakeware)
and voice (baker)
to transform the recipe
into a unique artisan loaf.

Bake on... Steve

Note from Steve

The no-knead bread method has revolutionized bread baking. The average family can now have fresh from the oven bakery quality artisan bread in the convenience of their own home with little or no-kneading... Mother Nature does the kneading for you. No-yeast proofing... instant yeast does not need to be proofed in warm water prior to using. No mixer... ingredients can be combined with a spoon. It's almost as easy as making a bowl of *Campbell's* soup.

This is "New Age Bread Baking". I understand what Italian bread, French bread, and baguettes are, and I understand the proper techniques for making those breads, but we live in a new age and we should embrace new ideas. Instead of trying to emulate bread methods of the past we should focus on our goal... to make great tasting, bakery quality, artisan bread with the methods and techniques that fit our busy schedules.

I believe in "Smart & Easy". Note, I didn't say fast and cheap. I make no-knead bread because it's the smartest, easiest, way to make bakery quality artisan bread and I believe my readers and subscribers are attracted to the no-knead method for the same reasons. In response to my readers and subscribers, I strive for convenience and address each recipe from a very practical standpoint... as, I believe, they would want me to develop my recipes.

I think you'll enjoy this cookbook.

Steve

Overview

There are three basic methods for making bread...
- **Knead by hand...** the most common method.
- **Bread machine...** very popular, but your loaf will have a silly little paddle in the bottom.
- **No-knead...** a method in which Mother Nature does the kneading for you.

This cookbook uses the "no-knead" method. The advantages are...
- **No kneading...** Mother Nature does the kneading for you.
- **No yeast proofing...** instant yeast doesn't require proofing.
- **No special equipment (no mixer, no bread machine)...** entire process is done in a glass bowl with a spoon and spatula, and can be baked in a wide variety of baking vessels (bread pan, uncovered baker, skillet, preheated Dutch oven, etc.).
- **Only 4 ingredients (flour, salt, yeast and water)...** to which other ingredients can be added to make a variety of specialty breads.

There are two methods for making no-knead bread...
- **Traditional...** proofs for 8 to 24 hours.
- **"Turbo"...** ready to bake in 2-1/2 hours.

This cookbook will start by teaching you how to make no-knead bread using the traditional method, then "Turbo" method, because the traditional method is more popular and a little easier.

What makes this cookbook different from others is...
- **"Hands-free technique"...** a new and innovative technique that uses the handle end of a plastic spoon to manipulate the dough (like a dough hook) after which the dough goes straight from the mixing bowl to the baking vessel (bread pan, etc.) without dusting the work surface with flour or touching the dough with your hands.
- **"Roll-to-coat"...** an innovative technique that coats the dough ball with flour in the mixing bowl. No more sticky dough. When the dough comes out of the bowl it will be easy to handle if you wish to divide the dough into portion to make baguettes, rolls, etc.

The cookbook also includes sections that will help you understand ingredients, technique, and bakeware.
- **Ingredients**
- **Technique & Tips**
- **Guide to Bread Pans**

Step by step, this cookbook will take you on a journey you will love and enjoy.

Ingredients

It only takes four ingredients to make bread... flour, salt, yeast and water.

Flour
Flour is the base ingredient of bread and there are four basic types of flour...

(1) Bread flour is designed for yeast bread. It has a higher percentage of gluten which gives artisan bread its airy crumb.

(2) All-purpose flour has less gluten than bread flour. I use all-purpose flour for biscuits, flatbreads, etc. In other words... I use it when I don't want an airy crumb.

(3) Self-rising flour is all-purpose flour with baking soda and baking powder added as leavening agents. It's intended for quick breads... premixed and ready to go. Do not use self-rising flour to make yeast bread. To see the difference between yeast and quick breads you may want to watch Introduction to No-Knead Beer Bread (a.k.a. Artisan Yeast Beer Bread) and Introduction to Quick Beer Bread (a.k.a. Beer Bread Dinner Rolls).

(4) And there are a variety of specialty flours... whole wheat, rye, and a host of others. Each has its unique flavor and characteristics. In some cases, you can substitute specialty flour for bread flour, but you may need to tweak the recipe because most specialty flours have less gluten. I frequently blend specialty flour with bread flour.

Flour is the primary ingredient... if you don't use the correct flour you won't get the desired results.

Note: To know how many cups of flour there are in a specific bag... it's typically on the side in "Nutritional Facts". For example, this bag reads, "Serving Size 1/4 cup... Serving Per Container about 75". In other words... 18.75 (75 times 1/4). That's the technical answer, but in the real world (measuring cup versus weight) a bag of flour will measure differently based on density (sifted versus unsifted), type of flour (wheat is more dense than bread flour), humidity (flour weighs more on humid days), and all the other variables life and nature have to offer. Thus, there is no single correct answer, but for practical purposes... figure a 5 lb bag of bread flour is 17 to 18 cups.

Salt
While it is possible to make bread without salt... you would be disappointed. There are three basics types of salt...

(1) Most baking recipes are designed to use everyday table salt unless specified otherwise. Unless you're experienced, it is probably smartest to use table salt for your baking needs.

(2) Kosher salt is excellent. I use it when I cook, but a tablespoon of kosher salt does not equal a tablespoon of table salt because kosher salt crystals are larger.

(3) And, I use specialty salt as a garnish... for appearance and taste. For example, I use sea salt to garnish pretzels.

Generally speaking, when salt is added as an ingredient and baked it is difficult to taste the difference between table, kosher and sea salt. When salt is added as a garnish and comes in contact with the taste buds... kosher or specialty salt is an excellent choice.

Yeast
Yeast is the "magic" ingredient which transforms flour and water into dough. Traditional no-knead recipes use 1/4 tsp yeast (we want the dough to rise slowly which allows the dough to develop flavor). "Turbo" recipes use 1-1/4 tsp yeast (ready to bake in 2-1/2 hours). There are three basic types of yeast...

(1) The most common is active dry yeast which is traditionally proofed in warm water prior to being added to flour.

(2) Instant dry yeast (a.k.a. "instant yeast", "bread machine yeast", "quick rise", "rapid rise", "fast rising", etc.) which was designed for bread machines and does not need to be proofed in warm water... why worry about proofing yeast if you don't have too.

(3) Some older recipes call for <u>cake yeast</u> (a.k.a. "compressed yeast" or "fresh yeast"), but it's perishable. You can substitute active and instant dry yeast for cake yeast when using older recipes.

Update: While I respect the history of bread making and opinions of others, I do all my own testing. And, when I designed "Turbo" bread I found proofing technique was more important than the amount of yeast. In other words... when I proofed at 78 to 85 degrees F. it didn't make any difference if I use 1-1/4 or 2-1/4 ounces yeast... I got the same results. The reason is... the manufacturing of yeast has significantly improved yeast (more live yeast and better strains) since the 1940's when recipes called for a 2-1/4 ounce packet of yeast. When you bake a lot, you can save a lot by reducing the amount is yeast.

Furthermore, because the quality of dry yeast has improved... I now believe active dry yeast and instant yeast are interchangeable. Active dry yeast is a different stain of yeast (designed to act faster), but for all practical purposes the results is very similar.

Water
Water hydrates the ingredients and activates the yeast. The no-knead method uses a little more water than the typical recipe... and that's a good thing. It makes it easier to combine the wet and dry ingredients, and contributes to its airy crumb.

(1) I use <u>tap water</u>. It's convenient and easy, but sometimes city water has too much chlorine (chlorine kills yeast).

(2) If your dough does not rise during first proofing you may want to use <u>bottled drinking water</u>.

(3) But, do not use <u>distilled water</u> because the minerals have been removed.

Water is a flavor ingredient, if your water doesn't taste good... use bottled drinking water.

Flavor Ingredients
It only takes four ingredients to make bread... flour, salt, yeast and water, to which a variety of flavor ingredients can be added to make specialty breads such as... honey whole wheat, multi-grain white, rosemary, Mediterranean olive, cinnamon raisin, honey oatmeal, and a host of others.

Technique & Tips

The techniques used to make traditional and "Turbo" no-knead bread are identical except proofing. Turbo uses shorter proofing times, thus it is important to use sound proofing technique (warm ingredients and a warm proofing environment) when using the "Turbo" method. The traditional method is demonstrated on YouTube in <u>No-Knead Bread 101 (Includes demonstration of Sesame Seed Bread... Italian, Muffuletta, & Sandwich)</u>. The "Turbo" method is demonstrated in <u>Ultimate Introduction to No-Knead "Turbo" Bread... ready to bake in 2-1/2 hours</u>. And my complete collection of videos is available at <u>http://nokneadbreadcentral.com/</u>.

Prep

Traditional: Because the traditional method proof for 8 to 24 hours it uses cool water to slow the proofing process, thus the temperature of the bowl is not important.

Turbo: To insure consistency and assist Mother Nature with proofing... it's important to provide yeast with a warm proofing environment (78 to 85% F). One of the keys to proofing temperature is the temperature of the mixing bowl because it has direct contact with the dough. Thus, I run the bowl under warm water so that it doesn't draw the heat out of the warm water.

Combining Ingredients

Pour water in a 3 to 4 qt glass mixing bowl (use warm water and a warm bowl for "Turbo" and cool for traditional). Add salt, yeast, flavor ingredients, etc... and stir to combine (it will insure the ingredients are evenly distributed). Add flour (flour will resist the water and float). Start by stirring the ingredients with the handle end of a plastic spoon drawing the flour from the sides into the middle of bowl (vigorously mixing will not hydrate the flour faster... but it will raise a lot of dust). Within 30 seconds the flour will hydrate and form a shaggy ball. Then scrape dry flour from side of bowl and tumble dough to combine moist flour with dry flour (about 15 seconds). It takes about one minute to combine wet and dry ingredients.

Traditional: Cover bowl with plastic wrap, place on counter, and proof for 8 to 24 hours.

Turbo: Cover bowl with plastic wrap, place in a warm draft free location, and proof for 1-1/2 hours.

1st Proofing (bulk fermentation)

The process is called "proofing" because it "proves" the yeast is active.

Bread making is nature at work (yeast is a living organism) and subject to nature. Seasons (summer vs. winter) and weather (heat & humidity) have a direct impact on proofing. In other words, don't worry if your dough varies in size... that's Mother Nature. Just focus on your goal... if the gluten forms (dough develops a stringy nature) and doubles in size... you're good to go.

If your dough does <u>not</u> rise the usual culprits are... outdated yeast or chlorinated water (chlorine kills yeast). Solution, get fresh yeast and/or use bottled drinking water.

If your dough is <u>slow</u> (takes "forever") to rise... your proofing temperature is probably too cool.

Traditional: Because the traditional method use long proofing times (8 to 24 hours) it does not require any special technique.

Turbo: Because "Turbo" dough use shorter proofing times (1-12/ hours) it is important to practice sound proofing technique.

The ideal temperature for proofing is 78 to 85 degrees F, but the typically home is 68 to 72 degrees, which is why recipes generally suggest proofing in a "warm draft-free environment". So, you have a choice... wait longer or create a warm proofing environment. My favorites are...

Oven setting: If your oven has a setting for proofing (80 degrees F)... use it.

Direct sunlight: Cover bowl with plastic wrap, place in direct sunlight, and the heat from the Sun will create a favorable proofing environment.

Oven light: If your oven has a light... cover bowl with plastic wrap, place in oven, turn light on, and close the door. The oven light will generate heat and increase the temperature inside the oven by several degrees. The amount of heat will depend on the size of the oven and strength of the bulb. The oven temperature will always start low and climb slowly, but it may go over 90 degrees F. so check periodically until you are familiar with the nature of your oven.

Desk Lamp: Cover bowl with plastic wrap, place under a desk lamp, lower lamp so that it's close to the bowl, and turn lamp on. The plastic wrap over the bowl will create a similar effect to leaving car windows rolled up on a sunny day.

Microwave: Place an 8 to 16 oz cup of water in the microwave and heat on high for 2 minutes. Then move the cup to the back corner, place mixing bowl (dough) in microwave and close the door. The heat and steam from the hot water will create a favorable environment for proofing.

Folding dough proofer: Commercial bakeries have large proofing ovens in which they can control climate and temperature. There are smaller versions available for the public that fold flat.

Tip: To fit bread making into your schedule… you can extend 1st proofing up to 4 hours (or even more), but don't shorten… it important to give Mother Nature time to form the gluten.

Degas, Pull & Stretch

The purpose of degassing, pulling and stretching is to, (a) expel the gases that formed during bulk fermentation, (b) strengthen the dough by realigning and stretching the gluten strands, and (c) stimulate yeast activity for 2nd proofing.

Because no-knead dough is sticky and difficult to handle… I degas, pull & stretch dough by stirring it in the bowl with the handle end of a plastic spoon (like a dough hook). It will reduce the size of the dough ball by 50% making it easier to handle and the process replaces folding and shaping in most cases.

Roll-to-Coat

Before removing the dough from bowl… dust the dough and side of the bowl with flour, then roll-to-coat. The flour will bond to the sticky dough making it easier to handle, but do not roll-to-coat with flour if you're going to garnish or baste.

Garnish & Baste

The purpose of garnishing and basting is to enhance the appearance of the crust, but it isn't necessary. If you decide to garnish and baste there are two techniques… roll-to-coat and skillet method.

Roll-to-Coat Method: Before removing dough from bowl… add ingredients to bowl (on the dough and side of the bowl), then roll to coat. For example, when I garnish honey oatmeal bread… I sprinkle oat in the bowl and on the dough, then roll the dough ball in the oats and they will bond to the sticky dough. This can also be done with seeds, grains, olive oil, egg wash, etc.

Skillet Method: When I want to garnish and/or baste the top of the loaf… I coat the proofing skillet with baste (egg wash, olive oil, vegetable oil, etc.) and sprinkle with the garnish (oats, seeds, grains, etc.). The ingredients will bond with the dough as the dough proofs.

Supporting video: How to Garnish & Baste No-Knead Bread using "Hands-Free" Technique

Divide & Shape

If you're not going to divide the dough… it can go straight from the mixing bowl to the proofing skillet or baking vessel. If you are going to divide and shape the dough… dust the dough and side of the bowl with flour and roll-to-coat, dust work surface with flour, roll the dough ball out of the bowl (excess flour and all) onto the work surface, and divide and shape. I use a plastic bowl scraper to assist in dividing, shaping and carry the dough to the baking vessel. Together they (flour & bowl scraper) make it easier to handle the dough.

2nd Proofing

Traditional: Originally I proofed for 1 to 2 hours, but over time I have been baking more in bread pans and found shorter proofing times gave better results. I now proof for 30 to 60 minutes.

Turbo: Place dough in a warm draft-free location and proof for 30 minutes.

Tip: To fit bread making into your schedule... you can extend 2nd proofing times, but you don't want the dough to exceed the size of the baking vessel. If you're using a large baking vessel (Dutch oven, etc.) it's never a problem, but if you're using a bread pan don't allow the dough to exceed the sides of the pan before baking or your loaf will droop over the sides and be less attractive. But, always bake it... it will still be delicious.

Score

The purpose of scoring dough is to provide seams to control where the crust will split during "oven spring", but it isn't necessary to score dough. If you do decide to score your loaf you may want to use a scissors (no-knead dough is very moist and more likely to stretch than slice). Personally, I place the dough in the baking vessel seam side up... the dough will split at the seam during "oven spring" which gives the loaf a nice rustic appearance.

Bake

Baking Time: Bread is done when it reaches an internal temperature of 185 to 220 degrees F. and the crumb (inside of the bread) isn't doughy. Baking times in my recipes are designed to give bread an internal temperature of 200 to 205 degrees F, but ovens vary and you may need to adjust your baking times slightly.

No-Stick Spray: Most bakeware has a non-stick surface, but it is safest to spray your bakeware unless you are fully confident your bread won't stick.

Ovens: Ovens aren't always accurate. I check the temperature of ovens and bakeware. Ovens with a digital readout that displays the temperature as they preheat are typically very accurate, but ovens that say they will be at temperature in a specific number of minutes are not always accurate. My point is... you will get the best results if you learn the character and nature of your oven.

Oven Rack: Generally speaking you want to bake bread and rolls in the middle or lower third of the oven, but it isn't critical. Just keep them away from the upper heating element or they may brown a little too quickly.

Oven Spring: When dough is first put into the oven it will increase in size by as much as a third in a matter of minutes because, (a) gases trapped in the dough will expand, (b) moisture will turn into steam and try to push its way out, and (c) yeast will become highly active converting sugars into gases. The steam and gases work together to create "oven spring". Once the internal temperature of the bread reaches 120 degrees F... the yeast will begin to die and the crust will harden.

Storing Bread & Dough

After allowing bread to cool... it can be wrapped in plastic wrap, or stored in a zip-lock plastic bag, or plastic bread bags (available on the web). If you wish to keep bread for a longer period of time... slice it into portions and freeze them in a zip-lock freezer bag (remove excess air). Do not store bread in the refrigerator. Bread goes stale faster in the refrigerator.

If you wish to save dough... divide it into portions, drizzle each portion with olive oil, place in zip-lock bag, remove excess air, and refrigerate for up to two days or freeze for up to two months. To thaw dough... move dough from freezer to refrigerator the day before (12 or more hours), then place on counter for 30 minutes before use to come to room temperature.

Equipment & Bakeware

Bowl for Mixing: You can use any 3 to 4 qt bowl. I use a 3-1/2 qt glass bowl because, (a) there's ample room for the dough to expand, (b) plastic wrap sticks to glass, and (c) I don't want the rim of my bowl to exceed the width of the plastic wrap.

Measuring Spoons: I'm sure you already have measuring spoons in the kitchen... they will work just fine. If you're going to buy new, I prefer oval versus round because an oval shape will fit into jars and containers more easily.

Measuring Cups: Dry measuring cups are designed to be filled to the top and leveled. Liquid measuring cups have a pour spout and are designed to be filled to the gradations on the side (neither measures weight). It is best to use the appropriate measuring cup.

Note: U.S. and metric measuring cups may be used interchangeably... there is only a slight difference (±3%). More importantly, the ingredients of a recipe measured with a set (U.S. or metric) will have their volumes in the same proportion to one another.

Spoon for Combining Wet and Dry Ingredients: A spoon is an excellent tool for combining wet and dry ingredients. Surprisingly, I found the handle end of a plastic spoon worked best for me because, I didn't have a big clump on the end like some of my other mixing utensils (which makes it easier to stir and manipulate the dough). And when you think about it... mixers don't use a paddle to mix dough, they use a hook which looks a lot like the handle end of my spoon.

Silicon Baking Mat: Silicone baking mats are very useful... I use them as reusable parchment paper (they're environmentally friendly). Silicone baking mats serve two purposes... (a) as a work surface for folding and shaping (they have excellent non-stick properties), and (b) as a baking mat... specifically when the dough is difficult to move after folding and shaping. And I slide a cookie sheet under the mat before baking (it makes it easier to put the mat into and take it out of the oven).

Spatula: I use a spatula to scrape the sides of the bowl to get the last bits of flour incorporated into the dough.

Plastic Bowl Scraper: I use a plastic bowl scraper verses a metal dough scraper because it's the better multi-tasker. I use the bowl scraper to (a) fold, shape, and divide the dough, (b) assist in transporting the dough to the proofing vessel, (c) scrape excess flour off the work surface, (d) scrape excess flour out of the bowl (after all it is a bowl scraper), and (e) scrape any remaining bits in the sink towards the disposal. It's a useful multi-tasker and you can't do all those tasks with a metal cough scraper.

Timer: I'm sure you already have a timer and it will work just fine. If you're thinking about a new one... I prefer digital because they're more accurate.

Proofing Baskets & Vessels: The purpose of a proofing basket or vessel is to pre-shape the dough prior to baking (dough will spread if it isn't contained). Because no-knead dough has a tendency to stick to the lining of proofing baskets... I use common household items as proofing vessels. For example, I use an 8" skillet (with no-stick spray) to pre-shape dough when baking in a Dutch oven. It shapes the dough during proofing, and the handle makes it easy to carry the dough and put it in the hot Dutch oven safely.

You can also proof dough in the baking vessel if it doesn't have to be preheated. For example, standard loaves are typically proof and baked in the bread pan where your bread pan shapes the loaf during proofing and baking. You can use this same principle for shaping and baking rolls and buns.

Baking Vessels: Baking vessels come in a variety of sizes, shapes and materials. You can change the appearance of the loaf by sampling changing the baking vessel.

Plastic Wrap & Proofing Towel: I use plastic wrap for 1st proofing and a lint-free towel for 2nd proofing. Plastic wrap protects dough for longer proofing times and can be used to create a favorable proofing environment (solar effect).

Cooling Rack: The purpose of a cooling rack is to expose the bottom of the loaf during the cooling process.

Bread Bags: I use plastic bread bags to store bread after they have cooled. And they're great for packaging bread as gifts. I also use paper bags as gifts when the loaf is still warm and I don't want to trap the moisture in a plastic bag... it gives a nice natural appearance.

10" Flat Whisk: I use a flat whisk to combine dry ingredients with yogurt... a flat whisk will slice through yogurt forming small clump. If you use a balloon whisk a big lump will form inside the balloon.

Pastry/Pizza Roller: When you watch shows they hand shape and toss pizza dough, but I find it more practical to use a pastry/pizza roller. It is also useful when shaping flatbread and cinnamon rolls.

Guide to Bread Pans

When I decided to bake no-knead bread in a bread pan, I felt it was important to test the options. Nothing earth-shaking, but a little general discussion may help you select the best pan for your intended purpose.

Basic Loaf Sizes

Loafs vary in size… some folks like larger loafs… some like smaller. No right… no wrong… it's personal taste. I like to use one pound of flour. A five pound bag of flour is typically 17 & 1/2 cups (3-1/2 cups per pound), which is why most of the recipes in this cookbook use 3-1/2 cups flour.

Basic Pan Sizes

Small (8" x 4"): Raisin bread is typically smaller than the other loaves. As a result, I use 3 cups flour (versus 3-1/2) and a smaller bread pan.

Medium (8-1/2" x 4-1/2") and Large (9" x 5"): These are the two most popular size bread pans. They are interchangeable… you can use either for all the recipes in this cookbook. The medium size loaf pan will give you a little taller loaf and the large will give you a little wider loaf.

Extra Large (9-1/2" x 5-1/2"): You may want to use 4 to 5 cups flour when baking in an extra large loaf pan.

Long (12" x 4-1/2"): The long bread pan is ideally suited for making long and half loaves.

Bottom-line: The medium (8-1/2" x 4-1/2") and large (9" x 5") bread pans are ideally suited for a one pound loaf (3-1/2 cups flour).

Types of Bread Pans

There are three basic types of loaf pans... standard, cast iron, and stoneware, glass, etc. Each manufacture claims to use the best material and design. I found 80% performed well and a few disappointed me.

I started my research by going to the manufacture's website to look at recipes and check on customer service. I will give the highest score to *USA Pans* and the lowest score to... well, I was disappointed with a fair number of the manufactures. Personally, I believe... if you're in the business of making bread pans you should offer recipes that maximize the value of your product and you should have a customer service link for feedback. In some cases I couldn't even locate the manufacturer.

Standard Loaf Pans

Standard loaf pans are the most popular... they're inexpensive and they perform well. Some manufacturers claim their dark loaf pans absorb radiant heat thus shortening baking time, while suggesting light colored shiny loaf pans reflect heat away, but I didn't find any loaf pan that reduced baking time (internal temperatures were all very similar after baking).

Good Cook **(8" x 4"):** Professional gauge steel nonstick medium loaf pan (Liquid Capacity: 42 oz | Weight: 8.0 oz). I was very pleased with the loaf pan and the size is ideally suited for those who want a small loaf. GoodCook.com is a good website, but the site does not have a recipe for standard yeast bread. It's inexpensive, an excellent value... excellent for home use.

USA Pan **(8-1/2" x 4-1/2"):** Silicone coated heavy gage aluminized steel nonstick loaf pan (Liquid Capacity: 48 oz | Weight: 1.0 lb). This is a heavy duty pan and its non-stick surface is among the best. USAPans.com is an excellent website and they were #1 in customer support. Excellent for home and professional use.

Chicago Metallic **(8-1/2" x 4-1/2"):** 26 gage aluminized steel diamond-quality nonstick loaf pan (Liquid Capacity: 50 oz | Weight: 12.75 oz). *Chicago Metallic* makes excellent bakeware. It's the workhorse found in many professional kitchens and its non-stick surface is excellent. ChicagoMetallicBakeware.com is a good website, but their recipes are limited and the site did not have a standard yeast bread recipe. They're excellent for home and professional use.

OXO **(8-1/2" x 4-1/2"):** *OXO* Good Gripe non-stick pro 1 lb loaf pan (Liquid capacity: 52 oz). The OXO is not in the picture because it was not available at the time of the test. It has become my favorite, but it is more expensive. Specifically, I like the rounded corners because they're easier to clean.

Good Cook (9" x 5"): Professional gauge steel nonstick large loaf pan (Liquid Capacity: 68 oz | Weight: 9.85 oz). I was very pleased with the loaf. GoodCook.com is a good website, but the site does not have a recipe for standard yeast bread. It's inexpensive, an excellent value... excellent for home use.

Bakersware (9" x 5"): "Bakersware" easy release surface loaf pan (Liquid Capacity: 62 oz | Weight: 7.3 oz). This is the only standard loaf pan I tested that wasn't metal. It's an excellent loaf pan. Bakersware.com is an excellent website (it answers your question without needing to ask) and the site has an excellent recipe for "Bachelor Bread". It's excellent for home and professional use, but it was the most expensive.

Note: Standard metal loaf pans are the most popular... they're inexpensive and perform well. In my tests they all preformed equally well (internal temperatures were all very similar after baking) except a thin super cheap one I tried and discarded. I like pans with handles and rounded corners... the handles make them easier to take out of the oven and the rounded corners are easier to clean.

Cast Iron

It's fun to bake with cast iron and it will give you an excellent loaf. Cast iron cost more than metal loaf pans, but they're not expensive.

Lodge **Cast Iron Loaf Pan (8-1/4" x 4-1/2"):** Pre-seasoned cast iron loaf pan (Liquid Capacity: 48 oz | Weight: 4 lb 3 oz). *Lodge* is slightly smaller than the other cast iron loaf pans, medium in weight, and has the most professional finish. LodgeMfg.com is a good website, but the site did not contain a standard yeast bread recipe. If you like baking with cast iron you'll love this loaf pan... excellent for home and professional use.

Camp Chef **Cast Iron Bread Pan (8-1/2" x 4-3/4"):** Cast iron true season finished bread pan (Liquid Capacity: 52 oz | Weight: 3 lb 3 oz). *Camp Chef* is medium in size and weight. The loaf was excellent, but the finish is rustic and hard to clean. CampChef.com is an average website, it has a lot of products, but it doesn't have recipes.

Old Mountain **Cast Iron Loaf Pan (8-1/2" x 5"):** Cast iron pre-seasoned loaf pan (Liquid Capacity: 54 oz | Weight: 5 lb 3 oz). *Old Mountain* is larger, heavier and is more rounded in shape. Its interior has a professional finish, but its exterior was more rustic. I was unable to find their website. Its tapered ends gave the loaf a unique shape... excellent for home and professional use.

Note: It's fun to bake with cast iron and it will give you an excellent loaf, but they are more expensive and the taste tasters couldn't tell the difference.

Stoneware, Glass, Etc.
Frequently we associate loaf pans with bread, but loaf pans are designed for a variety of uses (casseroles, meatloaf, etc.). I am very attracted to stoneware when can I bake & serve in them... they look terrific, but I never serve bread in the loaf pan. This is where it would have been helpful for the manufacture to offer recipes demonstrating the benefits of stoneware over less expensive bread pans.

Anchor Hocking **1.5 qt Glass Loaf Dish (9" x 5"):** Clear glass loaf dish (Liquid Capacity: 58 oz | Weight: 2 lb 12 oz). I was pleased with the loaf. AnchorHocking.com is a good website, addressed questions, but did not have recipes. It's a good value, but glass loaf pans brake, take longer to heat, and can give bread a soft bottom.

Giada de Laurentiis Ceramic Loaf Pan (9" x 5"): Ceramic loaf pan (Liquid Capacity: 64 oz | Weight: 3 lb 4 oz). I was very pleased with the loaf, but I could not find a website for the product. It's a very nice looking pan... excellent for home use, but not necessarily for bread baking.

Wilton **Indulgence Professional Stoneware (9" x 5"):** Professional stoneware (Liquid Capacity: 64 oz | Weight: 3 lb 5 oz). *Wilton* makes excellent bakeware and I have several of their pieces. Wilton.com is not my kind of website. Instead of recipes... they have a "recipe box" which requires your email address. It's a very nice looking pan... excellent for home use, but not necessarily for bread baking.

Haeger **Natural Stone Loaf Pan (9-1/2" x 5.25"):** Natural stone premium loaf pan (Liquid Capacity: 80 oz | Weight: 3 lb 4 oz). This is the loaf pan for which I had the highest expectations... it turned out to be my greatest disappointment. They claim... over time it "creates a cooking surface that releases food easily", but failed to provide instruction on how to season the loaf pan and I had serious problems with my loaves sticking. I typically use no-stick baking spray... the loaf bonded to the pan. I tried coating the bottom and sides with Crisco... the loaf bonded to the pan. The homepage was hard to find (it's HaegerPottery.com), their customer service did not meet my needs, and there were no recipes on their website. I followed up by checking customer satisfaction rating at various websites... and they do have a good following of satisfied customers... I'm not one of them.

"Traditional" No-Knead Bread... proofs 8 to 12 hours

There are two methods for making no-knead bread... "Traditional" (proofs for 8 to 24 hours) and "Turbo" (ready to bake in 2-1/2 hours). We'll start with the traditional because it is easier and more popular.

If you aren't familiar with my recipes and technique... you may want to watch: No-Knead Bread 101 (Includes demonstration of Sesame Seed Bread... Italian, Muffuletta, & Sandwich) and World's Easiest No-Knead Bread (Introducing "Hands-Free" Technique).

Country White Bread (First "traditional" loaf)
I picked this recipe to be your first loaf because it's the easiest... it has the fewest steps and it's baked in a bread pan. Here's how simple it is... combine ingredients in a glass bowl, mix with the handle end of a plastic spoon, cover with plastic wrap, and leave it on the counter to proof over night and it will be ready to bake in the morning at which time you will... spray a bread pan with no-stick spray, roll the dough out of the bowl into the pan, proof for 30 minutes, and bake. Simple, easy, fun.

What's new: This is the basic recipe using "hands-free technique". With minor changes in the following recipes you will be able to make a variety of breads.

Supporting video: World's Easiest No-Knead Bread (Introducing "Hands-Free" Technique)

Country White Bread... proof 8 to 24 hours

Pour water into a 3 to 4 qt glass mixing bowl.

 14 oz cool Water

Add salt and yeast... give a quick stir to combine.

 1-1/2 tsp Salt

 1/4 tsp Instant Yeast

Add flour... stir until dough forms a shaggy ball, scrape dry flour from side of bowl, then tumble dough to combine moist flour with dry flour.

 3-1/2 cups Bread Flour

Cover bowl with plastic wrap, place on counter, and proof for 8 to 24 hours.

8 to 24 hours later (bread pan)

When dough has risen and developed its gluten structure... spray the bread pan (8-1/2" x 4-1/2" or 9" x 5") with no-stick cooking spray and set aside.

"Degas, pull and stretch"... stick handle end of a plastic spoon in the dough and stir (dough will form a sticky ball). Then, scrape side of bowl to get remainder of the dough into the sticky dough ball.

Roll dough out of bowl into bread pan.

Place pan in a warm draft-free location, cover with a lint-free towel, and proof for 30 minutes.

Before dough is fully proofed...

Adjust oven rack so that the bread will be in the middle of the oven and pre-heat to 400 degrees F.

30 minutes later

When the dough has proofed and oven has come to temperature... place loaf pan in the oven and bake for 40 minutes.

40 minutes later

Remove bread pan from oven, gently turn loaf out on work surface and place on cooling rack.

Poof... you made your first no-knead bread.

Cheddar Cheese Bread (bread pan)
This is a gorgeous loaf and it's easy to make… just add cheese. It's something your parents and friends will love.

What's new: This recipe adds a flavor ingredient (cheese)… how simple is that. Flavor ingredients are added to either the wet or dry ingredients, depending on the nature of the flavor ingredient you're adding. And note, I used <u>coarsely</u> shredded Cheddar Cheese to create the speckled effect. Also note, the water was increased to compensate for the cheese.

Cheddar Cheese Bread

Pour water into a 3 to 4 qt glass mixing bowl.

> 16 oz cool Water

Add salt and yeast... give a quick stir to combine.

> 1-1/2 tsp Salt
>
> 1/4 tsp Instant Yeast

Add flour... then add cheese on top of the flour (if cheese is added before flour it will be harder to combine)... stir until dough forms a shaggy ball, scrape dry flour from side of bowl, then tumble dough to combine moist flour with dry flour.

> 3-1/2 cups Bread Flour
>
> 1 cup coarsely shredded Cheddar Cheese

Cover bowl with plastic wrap, place on counter, and proof for 8 to 24 hours.

8 to 24 hours later (bread pan)

When dough has risen and developed its gluten structure... spray the bread pan (8-1/2" x 4-1/2" or 9" x 5") with no-stick cooking spray and set aside.

"Degas, pull and stretch"... stick handle end of a plastic spoon in the dough and stir (dough will form a sticky ball). Then, scrape side of bowl to get remainder of the dough into the sticky dough ball.

Roll dough out of bowl into bread pan.

Place pan in a warm draft-free location, cover with a lint-free towel, and proof for 30 minutes.

Before dough is fully proofed...

Adjust oven rack so that the bread will be in the middle of the oven and pre-heat to 400 degrees F.

30 minutes later

When the dough has proofed and oven has come to temperature... place loaf pan in the oven and bake for 40 minutes.

40 minutes later

Remove bread pan from oven, gently turn loaf out on work surface and place on cooling rack.

Multigrain Country White Bread (bread pan)

This is one of my most popular loaves. My first multigrain loaves used 2 cups bread flour and 1 cup wheat flour. One time I forgot the wheat flour and used 3 cups bread flour. Surprise, surprise... the multigrain country white became one of my most popular breads. I had assumed those who liked grains also liked wheat breads, but there appears to be a significant segment of our society who likes multigrain bread without the wheat bread taste. Wheat is one of those things you either like or don't like, but it doesn't mean you don't like multigrain bread.

What's new: This recipe adds seeds and oats. The seeds are added to the wet ingredients and stirred to evenly distribute them. The oats are added on top of the dry ingredients to prevent them from absorbing the water before the flour. And note, the water was increased to compensate for the oats.

Multigrain Country White Bread

Pour water into a 3 to 4 qt glass mixing bowl.

     16 oz cool Water

Add salt, yeast, and seeds... give a quick stir to combine.

     1-1/2 tsp Salt
     1/4 tsp Instant Yeast
     1 Tbsp Sesame Seeds
     1 Tbsp Flax Seeds

Add flour... then add oats on top of the flour (if oats are added before flour they will absorb the water and it will be harder to combine)... stir until dough forms a shaggy ball, scrape dry flour from side of bowl, then tumble dough to combine moist flour with dry flour.

     3-1/2 cups Bread Flour
     1/2 cup Old Fashioned *Quaker* Oats

Cover bowl with plastic wrap, place on counter, and proof for 8 to 24 hours.

8 to 24 hours later (bread pan)

When dough has risen and developed its gluten structure... spray the bread pan (8-1/2" x 4-1/2" or 9" x 5") with no-stick cooking spray and set aside.

"Degas, pull and stretch"... stick handle end of a plastic spoon in the dough and stir (dough will form a sticky ball). Then, scrape side of bowl to get remainder of the dough into the sticky dough ball.

Roll dough out of bowl into bread pan.

Place pan in a warm draft-free location, cover with a lint-free towel, and proof for 30 minutes.

Before dough is fully proofed...

Adjust oven rack so that the bread will be in the middle of the oven and pre-heat to 400 degrees F.

30 minutes later

When the dough has proofed and oven has come to temperature... place loaf pan in the oven and bake for 40 minutes.

40 minutes later

Remove bread pan from oven, gently turn loaf out on work surface and place on cooling rack.

Honey Whole Wheat Bread (bread pan)
This recipe combines whole wheat flour with bread flour, which gives you the nutrition and nutty taste of whole wheat with the crumb of a Country White in a hearty loaf with a touch of honey for sweetness.

What's new: This recipe adds two flavor ingredients, olive oil and honey. They are added to the wet ingredients and stirred to combine. Then whole wheat flour is combined with bread flour to make your first wheat bread. The blending of flours will give the loaf a crumb (the inside of the bread).

Note: Make sure your wheat four is fresh (less than 6 months old) because whole wheat flour contains wheat germ... therefore oils... and the oils can make the flour rancid (not good eats) after six months.

Honey Whole Wheat Bread

Pour water into a 3 to 4 qt glass mixing bowl.

<u>16 oz cool Water</u>

Add salt, yeast, olive oil and honey... give a quick stir to combine.

<u>1-1/2 tsp Salt</u>
<u>1/4 tsp Instant Yeast</u>
<u>1 Tbsp extra-virgin Olive Oil</u>
<u>1 Tbsp Honey</u>

Add flour... stir until dough forms a shaggy ball, scrape dry flour from side of bowl, then tumble dough to combine moist flour with dry flour.

<u>2 cups Bread Flour</u>
<u>1-1/2 cups Whole Wheat Flour</u>

Cover bowl with plastic wrap, place on counter, and proof for 8 to 24 hours.

8 to 24 hours later (bread pan)

When dough has risen and developed its gluten structure... spray the bread pan (8-1/2" x 4-1/2" or 9" x 5") with no-stick cooking spray and set aside.

"Degas, pull and stretch"... stick handle end of a plastic spoon in the dough and stir (dough will form a sticky ball). Then, scrape side of bowl to get remainder of the dough into the sticky dough ball.

Roll dough out of bowl into bread pan.

Place pan in a warm draft-free location, cover with a lint-free towel, and proof for 30 minutes.

Before dough is fully proofed...

Adjust oven rack so that the bread will be in the middle of the oven and pre-heat to 400 degrees F.

30 minutes later

When the dough has proofed and oven has come to temperature... place loaf pan in the oven and bake for 40 minutes.

40 minutes later

Remove bread pan from oven, gently turn loaf out on work surface and place on cooling rack.

No-Knead "Turbo" Bread... ready to bake in 2-1/2 hours

Now that you have mastered traditional no-knead bread... it's time to learn how to make no-knead bread that will be ready to bake in 2-1/2 hours. It was designed for those who want to make no-knead bread, but... don't want to wait 8 to 24 hours. For those who want bread machine bread, but... don't want to buy and store a bread machine.

There are two changes... ingredients and sound proofing technique.

Ingredients
Yeast is the active ingredient that makes the dough rise, thus shorter proofing times require more yeast. As a result, the recipe calls for 1-1/4 teaspoons yeast.

Sound proofing technique
Use a warm bowl, warm ingredients and warm proofing environment. The ideal temperature for proofing is 78 to 85 degrees F, but the typically home is 68 to 72 degrees, which is why recipes generally suggest proofing in a "warm draft-free environment". So, you have a choice... wait longer for the dough to proof or create a warm proofing environment. My favorite techniques for creating a warm proofing environment are...

Oven setting: If your oven has a setting for proofing (80 degrees F)... use it.

Direct sunlight: Cover bowl with plastic wrap, place in direct sunlight, and the heat from the Sun will create a more favorable proofing environment.

Oven light: If your oven has a light... cover bowl with plastic wrap, place in oven, turn light on, and close the door. The oven light will generate heat and increase the temperature inside the oven by several degrees. The amount of heat will depend on the size of the oven and strength of the bulb. The oven temperature will start low and climb slowly. Each oven is different, so check periodically until you are familiar with the nature of your oven.

Desk Lamp: Cover bowl with plastic wrap, place under a desk lamp, lower lamp so that it's close to the bowl, and turn lamp on. The plastic wrap over the bowl will create a similar effect to leaving car windows rolled up on a sunny day.

Supporting video: How to Proof Bread Dough (a.k.a. The Dynamics of Proofing)

Country White "Turbo" Bread (First "Turbo" loaf)
This is the same loaf as the traditional Country White Bread using the "Turbo" method (ingredients & technique). They will look and taste the same.

What's new: This recipe shows you how to make no-knead bread in less time... 2-1/2 hours verses 8 to 24 hours. Three things... (a) use a warm bowl and warm ingredients (warm temperatures encourage yeast activity), (b) use 1-1/4 tsp yeast verses 1/4 tsp yeast (shorter proofing times need additional yeast), and (c) it very important to proof in a warm, draft-free, environment (78 to 85 degrees).

Important note: You can apply the "Turbo" technique to any of my recipes. The ingredients are independent of the method.

Country White Bread... ready to bake in 2-1/2 hours

Pour warm water in a 3 to 4 qt warm glass mixing bowl (use a warm bowl... you don't want a cold bowl to take the heat out of the warm water).

<u>14 oz warm Water</u>

Add salt and yeast... give a quick stir to combine.

<u>1-1/2 tsp Salt</u>
<u>1-1/4 tsp Instant Yeast</u>

Add flour... stir until dough forms a shaggy ball, scrape dry flour from side of bowl, then tumble dough to combine moist flour with dry flour.

<u>3-1/2 cups Bread Flour</u>

Cover bowl with plastic wrap, place in a warm draft-free location, and proof for 1-1/2 hours.

1-1/2 hours later (bread pan)

When dough has risen and developed its gluten structure... spray the bread pan (8-1/2" x 4-1/2" or 9" x 5") with no-stick cooking spray and set aside.

"Degas, pull and stretch"... stick handle end of a plastic spoon in the dough and stir (dough will form a sticky ball). Then, scrape side of bowl to get remainder of the dough into the sticky dough ball.

Roll dough out of bowl into bread pan.

Place pan in a warm draft-free location, cover with a lint-free towel, and proof for 30 minutes.

Before dough is fully proofed...

Adjust oven rack so that the bread will be in the middle of the oven and pre-heat to 400 degrees F.

30 minutes later

When the dough has proofed and oven has come to temperature... place loaf pan in the oven and bake for 40 minutes.

40 minutes later

Remove bread pan from oven, gently turn loaf out on work surface and place on cooling rack.

Country White Bread (bread pan... garnished with sesame seeds)
Garnishing a loaf with sesame seeds is easy and it gives the loaf a special appearance.

What's new: This recipe demonstrates how to use the "roll-to-coat" technique to garnish the crust.

No-knead dough is very sticky... this techniques takes advantage of the sticky dough. After proofing... (a) stick the handle end of the plastic spoon in the dough and stir (the dough will form a sticky ball), (b) scrape the side of the bowl to get the remainder of the dough into the sticky dough ball, then (c) sprinkle 2 Tbsp of sesame seeds on the dough ball and side of the bowl, and use the spoon handle to roll the dough in the seeds (the seeds will bond to the sticky dough). Poof, you've garnished your loaf with sesame seeds.

Country White Bread - garnished with sesame seeds

Pour warm water in a 3 to 4 qt warm glass mixing bowl (use a warm bowl... you don't want a cold bowl to take the heat out of the warm water).

<u>14 oz warm Water</u>

Add salt and yeast... give a quick stir to combine.

<u>1-1/2 tsp Salt</u>
<u>1-1/4 tsp Instant Yeast</u>

Add flour... stir until dough forms a shaggy ball, scrape dry flour from side of bowl, then tumble dough to combine moist flour with dry flour.

<u>3-1/2 cups Bread Flour</u>

Cover bowl with plastic wrap, place in a warm draft-free location, and proof for 1-1/2 hours.

1-1/2 hours later (bread pan - garnish)

When dough has risen and developed its gluten structure... spray the bread pan (8-1/2" x 4-1/2" or 9" x 5") with no-stick cooking spray and set aside.

"Degas, pull and stretch"... stick handle end of a plastic spoon in the dough and stir (dough will form a sticky ball). Then, scrape side of bowl to get remainder of the dough into the sticky dough ball.

Garnish... sprinkle dough ball and side of bowl with sesame seeds and roll-to-coat (roll dough ball in sesame seeds to coat).

<u>2 Tbsp Sesame Seeds</u>

Roll dough out of bowl into bread pan.

Place pan in a warm draft-free location, cover with a lint-free towel, and proof for 30 minutes.

Before dough is fully proofed...

Adjust oven rack so that the bread will be in the middle of the oven and pre-heat to 400 degrees F.

30 minutes later

When the dough has proofed and oven has come to temperature... place loaf pan in the oven and bake for 40 minutes.

40 minutes later

Remove bread pan from oven, gently turn loaf out on work surface and place on cooling rack.

Multigrain Country White Bread (bread pan... garnished with oats)

Wow, this is a gorgeous loaf with flavor to match. It's hard to believe it was made in a glass bowl with a spoon.

What's new: This recipe adds seeds to the wet ingredients, oats to the dry ingredients (just like Multigrain Country White Bread), then it's garnished with oats. To garnish... (a) stick the handle end of the plastic spoon in the dough and stir (dough will form a sticky ball), (b) scrape the side of the bowl to get the remainder of the dough into the sticky dough ball, (c) sprinkle 1/4 cup Old Fashioned *Quaker* Oats on the dough ball and side of the bowl, then use the spoon handle to roll the dough in the oats. It's that simple.

Multigrain Country White Bread - garnished with oats

Pour warm water in a 3 to 4 qt warm glass mixing bowl (use a warm bowl... you don't want a cold bowl to take the heat out of the warm water).

<u>16 oz warm Water</u>

Add salt, yeast and seeds... give a quick stir to combine.

<u>1-1/2 tsp Salt</u>
<u>1-1/4 tsp Instant Yeast</u>
<u>1 Tbsp Sesame Seeds</u>
<u>1 Tbsp Flax Seeds</u>

Add flour... then oats (if oats are added before flour they will absorb the water and it will be harder to combine)... stir until dough forms a shaggy ball, scrape dry flour from side of bowl, then tumble dough to combine moist flour with dry flour.

<u>3-1/2 cups Bread Flour</u>
<u>1/2 cup Old Fashioned *Quaker* Oats</u>

Cover bowl with plastic wrap, place in a warm draft-free location, and proof for 1-1/2 hours.

1-1/2 hours later (bread pan - garnish)

When dough has risen and developed its gluten structure... spray the bread pan (8-1/2" x 4-1/2" or 9" x 5") with no-stick cooking spray and set aside.

"Degas, pull and stretch"... stick handle end of a plastic spoon in the dough and stir (dough will form a sticky ball). Then, scrape side of bowl to get remainder of the dough into the sticky dough ball.

Garnish... sprinkle dough ball and side of bowl with oats, and roll-to-coat (roll dough ball in oats to coat).

<u>1/4 cup Old Fashioned *Quaker* Oats</u>

Roll dough out of bowl into bread pan.

Place pan in a warm draft-free location, cover with a lint-free towel, and proof for 30 minutes.

Before dough is fully proofed...

Adjust oven rack so that the bread will be in the middle of the oven and pre-heat to 400 degrees F.

30 minutes later

When the dough has proofed and oven has come to temperature... place loaf pan in the oven and bake for 40 minutes.

40 minutes later

Remove bread pan from oven, gently turn loaf out on work surface and place on cooling rack.

Congratulations... You're a Master Baker!

You have learned all the basic techniques. You can make traditional no-knead bread (proofs for 8 to 24 hours) and no-knead "Turbo" bread (ready to bake in 2-1/2 hours). You have learned how to add flavor ingredients to both wet and dry ingredients, and you have learned how to garnish no-knead bread. My dear friends... you're a master baker. If you put one of your loaves on the shelf next to the artisan bread in a grocery store... your neighbor would not know the difference.

And it's important to remember... recipes are independent of method. You can take any of my recipes and use the traditional or "Turbo" method. And, you can garnish or not garnish any loaf. It's optional. You're the baker... you decide.

Additional Recipes

And it's important to remember… recipes are independent of method. You can take any of my recipes and use the traditional or "Turbo" method. And, you can garnish or not garnish any loaf. It's optional. You're the baker… you decide.

Here are a few more recipes.

Beer Bread (bread pan)
The purpose of this recipe is to introduce those of you who make beer bread to the no-knead method of making dough and introduce those of you who make no-knead bread to beer bread. One simple recipe with hundreds of options... change the wet ingredient—the beer—from a lager, to an amber, or a hefeweizen you can have a new and uniquely flavored bread. It's fun to experiment with beer bread and the beer isle is full of ideas.

There are two basic types of beer bread... yeasted and quick. Yeasted beer bread uses yeast as a leavening agent. The yeast gives the loaf an airy crumb and artisan quality. Quick beer bread uses self rising flour which has baking soda and baking powder as leavening agents. Quick beer bread is—as the name implies—very quick and easy, but don't let that fool you. It makes delicious rolls. To see the difference you may want to watch, Introduction to No-Knead Beer Bread (a.k.a. Artisan Yeast Beer Bread) and Introduction to Quick Beer Bread (a.k.a. Beer Bread Dinner Rolls).

Options:
"Turbo" method... if you wish to reduce the proofing time from 8 hours to 1-1/2 hours... increase yeast from 1/4 tsp yeast to 1-1/4 tsp and proof in a warm draft free environment (78 to 85 degrees F).

Beer Bread

Pour beer into a 3 to 4 qt glass mixing bowl.

    14 oz Beer

Add salt and yeast... give a quick stir to combine.

    1-1/2 tsp Salt

    1/4 tsp Instant Yeast

Add flour... stir until dough forms a shaggy ball, scrape dry flour from side of bowl, then tumble dough to combine moist flour with dry flour.

    3-1/2 cups Bread Flour

Cover bowl with plastic wrap, place on counter, and proof for 8 to 24 hours.

8 to 24 hours later (bread pan)

When dough has risen and developed its gluten structure... spray the bread pan (8-1/2" x 4-1/2" or 9" x 5") with no-stick cooking spray and set aside.

"Degas, pull and stretch"... stick handle end of a plastic spoon in the dough and stir (dough will form a sticky ball). Then, scrape side of bowl to get remainder of the dough into the sticky dough ball.

Roll dough out of bowl into bread pan.

Place pan in a warm draft-free location, cover with a lint-free towel, and proof for 30 minutes.

Before dough is fully proofed...

Adjust oven rack so that the bread will be in the middle of the oven and pre-heat to 400 degrees F.

30 minutes later

When the dough has proofed and oven has come to temperature... place loaf pan in the oven and bake for 40 minutes.

40 minutes later

Remove bread pan from oven, gently turn loaf out on work surface and place on a cooling rack.

Honey Oatmeal Bread (bread pan | garnish)

Fresh from the oven bread with the wholesome goodness of oats and the sweetness of honey... what's not to like? This loaf is as delicious to eat as it is pleasing to the eye.

Options:

"Turbo" method... if you wish to reduce the proofing time from 8 hours to 1-1/2 hours... increase yeast from 1/4 tsp yeast to 1-1/4 tsp and proof in a warm draft free environment (78 to 85 degrees F).

Honey Oatmeal Bread

Pour water into a 3 to 4 qt glass mixing bowl.

> 16 oz cool Water

Add salt, yeast, and honey... give a quick stir to combine.

> 1-1/2 tsp Salt
>
> 1/4 tsp Instant Yeast
>
> 1 Tbsp Honey

Add flour... then oats (if oats are added before flour they will absorb the water and it will be harder to combine)... stir until dough forms a shaggy ball, scrape dry flour from side of bowl, then tumble dough to combine moist flour with dry flour.

> 3-1/2 cups Bread Flour
>
> 1 cup Old Fashioned Quaker Oats

Cover bowl with plastic wrap, place on counter, and proof for 8 to 24 hours.

8 to 24 hours later (bread pan | garnish)

When dough has risen and developed its gluten structure... spray the bread pan (8-1/2" x 4-1/2" or 9" x 5") with no-stick cooking spray and set aside.

"Degas, pull and stretch"... stick handle end of a plastic spoon in the dough and stir (the dough will form a sticky ball). Then, scrape the side of the bowl to get the remainder of the dough into the sticky dough ball.

Garnish... sprinkle dough ball and side of bowl with oats, and roll-to-coat (roll dough ball in oats to coat).

> 1/4 cup Old Fashioned *Quaker* Oats

Roll dough out of bowl into bread pan.

Place pan in a warm draft-free location, cover with a lint-free towel, and proof for 30 minutes.

Before dough is fully proofed...

Adjust oven rack so that the bread will be in the middle of the oven and pre-heat to 400 degrees F.

30 minutes later

When the dough has proofed and oven has come to temperature... place loaf pan in the oven and bake for 40 minutes.

40 minutes later

Remove bread pan from oven, gently turn loaf out on work surface and place on a cooling rack.

Harvest 8 Grain Whole Wheat Bread (bread pan)

This Harvest 8 Grain Wheat Bread has a more robust and complex flavor than the multigrain country white and wheat breads. I experimented with and tested a number of my own multigrain mixtures before I discovered King Arthur's Harvest Grains Blend and (as they state on their website) the whole oat berries, millet, rye flakes and wheat flakes enhance texture while the flax, poppy, sesame, and sunflower seeds add crunch and great, nutty flavor. Wow, the flavor is great... and it's a lot easier and... more practical... to purchase a blend of seeds. You should experiment with blends available in your community.

Notes: Because whole wheat flour has less gluten... 100% whole wheat loaves can be a little too heavy and dense for some tastes. Personally, I like to balance the nutritional value of whole wheat with the crumb and texture of a Country White by using a blend.

Options:
"Turbo" method... if you wish to reduce the proofing time from 8 hours to 1-1/2 hours... increase yeast from 1/4 tsp yeast to 1-1/4 tsp and proof in a warm draft free environment (78 to 85 degrees F).

Harvest 8 Grain Whole Wheat Bread

Pour water into a 3 to 4 qt glass mixing bowl.

16 oz cool Water

Add salt, yeast, olive oil and grains... give a quick stir to combine.

1-1/2 tsp Salt

1/4 tsp Instant Yeast

1 Tbsp extra-virgin Olive Oil

2/3 cup King Arthur Harvest Grains Blend

Add flour... stir until dough forms a shaggy ball, scrape dry flour from side of bowl, then tumble dough to combine moist flour with dry flour.

2 cups Bread Flour

1-1/2 cups Whole Wheat Flour

Cover bowl with plastic wrap, place on counter, and proof for 8 to 24 hours.

8 to 24 hours later (bread pan)

When dough has risen and developed its gluten structure... spray the bread pan (8-1/2" x 4-1/2" or 9" x 5") with no-stick cooking spray and set aside.

"Degas, pull and stretch"... stick handle end of a plastic spoon in the dough and stir (the dough will form a sticky ball). Then, scrape the side of the bowl to get the remainder of the dough into the sticky dough ball.

Roll dough out of bowl into bread pan.

Place pan in a warm draft-free location, cover with a lint-free towel, and proof for 30 minutes.

Before dough is fully proofed...

Adjust oven rack so that the bread will be in the middle of the oven and pre-heat to 400 degrees F.

30 minutes later

When the dough has proofed and oven has come to temperature... place loaf pan in the oven and bake for 40 minutes.

40 minutes later

Remove bread pan from oven, gently turn loaf out on work surface and place on a cooling rack.

Deli Rye Bread (bread pan)
This is a rustic rye bread, with a mild rye flavor and a generous amount of caraway seeds that would be the perfect complement to a pastrami sandwich.

YouTube Video in support of recipe: World's Easiest No-Knead Deli Rye Bread (no mixer... "hands-free" technique) (July 2016 - 6:51)

Options:
"Turbo" method... if you wish to reduce the proofing time from 8 hours to 1-1/2 hours... increase yeast from 1/4 tsp yeast to 1-1/4 tsp and proof in a warm draft free environment (78 to 85 degrees F).

Deli Rye Bread

Pour water into a 3 to 4 qt glass mixing bowl.

    14 oz cool Water

Add salt, yeast, sugar, olive oil and seeds... give a quick stir to combine.

    1-1/2 tsp Salt
    1/4 tsp Instant Yeast
    1 Tbsp Sugar
    2 Tbsp Caraway Seeds
    1 Tbsp extra-virgin Olive Oil

Add flour... stir until dough forms a shaggy ball, scrape dry flour from side of bowl, then tumble dough to combine moist flour with dry flour.

    2-1/2 cups Bread Flour
    1 cup Rye Flour

Cover bowl with plastic wrap, place on counter, and proof for 8 to 24 hours.

8 to 24 hours later (bread pan)

When dough has risen and developed its gluten structure... spray the bread pan (8-1/2" x 4-1/2" or 9" x 5") with no-stick cooking spray and set aside.

"Degas, pull and stretch"... stick handle end of a plastic spoon in the dough and stir (the dough will form a sticky ball). Then, scrape the side of the bowl to get the remainder of the dough into the sticky dough ball.

Roll dough out of bowl into bread pan.

Place pan in a warm draft-free location, cover with a lint-free towel, and proof for 30 minutes.

Before dough is fully proofed...

Adjust oven rack so that the bread will be in the middle of the oven and pre-heat to 400 degrees F.

30 minutes later

When the dough has proofed and oven has come to temperature... place loaf pan in the oven and bake for 40 minutes.

40 minutes later

Remove bread pan from oven, gently turn loaf out on work surface and place on a cooling rack.

Mediterranean Olive Bread (long loaf pans | half loaves | baste)
If you like Mediterranean flavors you'll love this bread. It's perfect with cream cheese, pimento cheese spread, deli meat & provolone, etc. It's unique... it's different... it's perfect for that special occasion. If a restaurant served you this loaf as their signature bread... you'd be talking about it for years and you'd be surprised how easy it is to make.

Options:
"Turbo" method... if you wish to reduce the proofing time from 8 hours to 1-1/2 hours... increase yeast from 1/4 tsp yeast to 1-1/4 tsp and proof in a warm draft free environment (78 to 85 degrees F).

Mediterranean Olive Bread

Prepare flavor ingredients... zest lemon, slice green olives in half, slice kalamata olives in thirds, and set aside.

> Zest of 1 Lemon
> 2-1/4 oz (1 can) sliced Black Olives
> 1 can stuffed Green Olives (use black olive can to measure)
> 1 can pitted Kalamata Olives (use black olive can to measure)

Pour water into a 3 to 4 qt glass mixing bowl.

> 14 oz cool Water

Add salt, yeast, thyme, and olive oil... give a quick stir to combine.

> 1-1/2 tsp Salt
> 1/4 tsp Instant Yeast
> 1 tsp dried Thyme
> 1 Tbsp extra-virgin Olive Oil

Add flour... then flavor ingredients. Stir until dough forms a shaggy ball, scrape dry flour from side of bowl, then tumble dough to combine moist flour with dry flour.

> 3-1/2 cups Bread Flour

Cover bowl with plastic wrap, place on counter, and proof for 8 to 24 hours.

8 to 24 hours later (long loaf pans | half loaves | baste)

When dough has risen and developed its gluten structure... spray 2 long loaf pans with no-stick cooking spray and set aside.

"Degas, pull and stretch"... stick handle end of a plastic spoon in the dough and stir (the dough will form a sticky ball). Then, scrape the side of the bowl to get the remainder of the dough into the sticky dough ball.

Baste... drizzle dough and side of bowl with olive oil... roll dough in oil to coat.

> 1 to 2 Tbsp Olive Oil

Roll dough out of bowl onto work surface.

Divide dough into 2 portions, roll on work surface to shape, and place in pans.

Place pan in a warm draft-free location, cover with a lint-free towel, and proof for 30 minutes.

Before dough is fully proofed...

Adjust oven rack so that the bread will be in the middle of the oven and pre-heat to 400 degrees F.

30 minutes later

When the dough has proofed and oven has come to temperature... place loaf pan in the oven and bake for 35 minutes.

35 minutes later

Remove bread pan from oven, gently turn loaf out on work surface and place on a cooling rack.

Cinnamon Raisin Bread (small bread pan)
Homemade fresh from the oven cinnamon raisin bread is a great way to start your day and when our guests stay overnight, my wife wants them to wake up to the aroma of fresh for the oven cinnamon raisin bread filling the house.

Note: Raisin bread is ideally suited for a smaller loaf pan. Because cinnamon retards yeast activity... this recipe requires additional yeast (2-1/4 vs. 1-1/4 tsp) and it is very important to proof in a warm (78 to 85 degrees F) proofing environment.

Optional:
Traditional method... if you wish to use the traditional method... decrease yeast from 2-1/4 tsp to 1-1/4 tsp and proof 8 to 24 hours.

Cinnamon Raisin Bread

Pour warm water in a 3 to 4 qt warm glass mixing bowl (use a warm bowl... you don't want a cold bowl to take the heat out of the warm water).

> 14 oz warm Water

Add salt, yeast, sugar, and cinnamon... give a quick stir to combine with a flat whisk or fork (it will make it easier to combine the cinnamon).

> 1-1/2 tsp Salt
> 2-1/4 tsp Instant Yeast
> 2 Tbsp Brown Sugar
> 1 Tbsp ground Cinnamon

Add flour... then raisins. Stir until dough forms a shaggy ball, scrape dry flour from side of bowl, then tumble dough to combine moist flour with dry flour.

> 3 cups Bread Flour
> 1 cup Raisins

Cover bowl with plastic wrap, place in a warm draft-free location, and proof for 1-1/2 hours.

1-1/2 hours later (small bread pan)

When dough has risen and developed its gluten structure... spray the bread pan (8" x 4") with no-stick cooking spray and set aside.

"Degas, pull and stretch"... stick handle end of a plastic spoon in the dough and stir (the dough will form a sticky ball). Then, scrape the side of the bowl to get the remainder of the dough into the sticky dough ball.

Roll dough out of bowl into bread pan.

Place pan in a warm draft-free location, cover with a lint-free towel, and proof for 30 minutes.

Before dough is fully proofed...

Adjust oven rack so that the bread will be in the middle of the oven and pre-heat to 400 degrees F.

30 minutes later

When the dough has proofed and oven has come to temperature... place loaf pan in the oven and bake for 45 minutes (typically I would bake a standard 3 cup loaf in a 4" x 8" bread pan for 35 minutes, but raisin bread may need to be baked for an additional 5 to 10 minutes because of the moisture and density of the raisins).

45 minutes later

Remove bread pan from oven, gently turn loaf out on work surface and place on a cooling rack.

Italian Sesame Sandwich Bread (poor man's Dutch oven)
For the Italian sesame sandwich bread I used a "poor-man's-Dutch oven" (PMDO). It's the best of both worlds… the shape of sandwich bread using the principles of a Dutch oven. I used two 8-1/2" x 4-1/2" OXO bread pans, but 9" x 5" pans are perfectly acceptable.

YouTube Video in support of recipe: No-Knead Bread 101 (Includes demonstration of Sesame Seed Bread… Italian, Muffuletta, & Sandwich) (June 17, 2016 – 14:23)

Optional:
Traditional method… if you wish to use the traditional method… decrease yeast from 1-1/4 tsp to 1/4 tsp and proof 8 to 24 hours.
Add sesame and flax seed to dough… you can create an interesting appearance, texture and flavor by adding 1 Tbsp (each) sesame and flax seeds to the dough.

Italian Sesame Sandwich Bread

Pour warm water in a 3 to 4 qt warm glass mixing bowl (use a warm bowl... you don't want a cold bowl to take the heat out of the warm water).

> 14 oz warm Water

Add salt, yeast and olive oil... give a quick stir to combine.

> 1-1/2 tsp Salt
>
> 1-1/4 tsp Instant Yeast
>
> 1 Tbsp Extra Virgin Olive Oil
>
> 1 Tbsp Sesame Seeds (optional)

Add flour... stir until dough forms a shaggy ball, scrape dry flour from side of bowl, then tumble dough to combine moist flour with dry flour.

> 3-1/2 cups Bread Flour

Cover bowl with plastic wrap, place in a warm draft-free location, and proof for 1-1/2 hours.

1-1/2 hours later (PMDO - garnish)

When dough has risen and developed its gluten structure... spray bottom pan (8-1/2" x 4-1/2" or 9" x 5") with no-stick cooking spray and set aside.

"Degas, pull and stretch"... stick handle end of a plastic spoon in the dough and stir (the dough will form a sticky ball). Then, scrape the side of the bowl to get the remainder of the dough into the sticky dough ball.

Garnish... sprinkle dough ball and side of bowl with sesame seeds and roll-to-coat (roll dough ball in sesame seeds to coat).

> 2 Tbsp Sesame Seeds

Roll dough out of bowl into bread pan.

Cover bottom bread pan with top pan and place in a warm draft-free location to proof for 30 minutes.

Before dough is fully proofed...

Move rack to lower third of oven and pre-heat to 400 degrees F.

30 minutes later

When the dough has proofed and oven has come to temperature... place PMDO in oven and bake for 40 minutes.

40 minutes later

Remove PMDO from oven, remove the top, and place pan back in the oven for 3 to 15 minutes to finish the crust.

3 to 15 minutes later

Gently turn loaf out on work surface and place on cooling rack.

Garlic Bread (poor man's Dutch oven | long loaf pans)
All of us like garlic cheese bread... I like to lightly infuse the garlic into the loaf. It gives the loaf a nice full flavor and it's easier than adding garlic after the fact.

Note: This recipe calls for 1 to 2 heaping tsp minced garlic (jar). I generally use 1, but it's a personal taste issue. Try both and see which you like.

I used two *Wilton* 12" x 4-1/2" long bread pans for my "poor man's Dutch oven".

Picture: As an appetizer for dinner I served garlic cheese bread. Because the garlic is already infused in the bread, all I needed to do was... toast two slices, spread on a little butter, add a little cheese, a sprinkle of salt, and broil them in the toaster oven to melt the cheese.

Options:
Standard vs. long PMDO... use the same ingredients and increase baking time by 5 minutes.
"Turbo" method... if you wish to reduce the proofing time from 8 hours to 1-1/2 hours... increase yeast from 1/4 tsp yeast to 1-1/4 tsp and proof in a warm draft free environment (78 to 85 degrees F).

Garlic Bread

Pour water into a 3 to 4 qt glass mixing bowl.

     <u>14 oz cool Water</u>

Add salt, yeast, garlic and olive oil... give a quick stir to combine.

     <u>1-1/2 tsp Salt</u>

     <u>1/4 tsp Instant Yeast</u>

     <u>1 to 2 heaping tsp Minced Garlic (jar)</u>

     <u>1 Tbsp extra-virgin Olive Oil</u>

Add flour... stir until dough forms a shaggy ball, scrape dry flour from side of bowl, then tumble dough to combine moist flour with dry flour.

     <u>3-1/2 cups Bread Flour</u>

Cover with plastic wrap and place in a warm draft-free location to proof for 8 to 24 hours.

8 to 24 hours later (PMDO | long loaf pans)

When dough has risen and developed its gluten structure... spray bottom long loaf pan (12" x 4-1/2") with no-stick cooking spray and set pans aside.

"Degas, pull and stretch"... stick handle end of a plastic spoon in the dough and stir (the dough will form a sticky ball). Then, scrape the side of the bowl to get the remainder of the dough into the sticky dough ball.

"Roll-to-coat"... sprinkle dough ball and side of bowl with flour and roll-to-coat (dusting dough ball with flour will make it easier to handle and shape the dough for the baker).

     <u>2 Tbsp Bread Flour</u>

Dust work surface with flour, roll dough (and excess flour) out of bowl onto work surface, roll dough on work surface in flour to shape, and place in baker.

Cover bottom bread pan with top pan and place in a warm draft-free location to proof for 30 minutes.

Before dough is fully proofed...

Move oven rack to lower third of the oven and pre-heat to 400 degrees F.

30 minutes later

When the dough has proofed and oven has come to temperature... place PMDO in oven and bake for 35 minutes with the top on.

35 minutes later

Take PMDO out of the oven, remove top, and place back in the oven for 3 to 15 minutes to finish the crust... depending on how rustic (hard) you like your crust.

3 to 15 minutes later

Remove baker from oven, gently turn loaf out on work surface and place on a cooling rack.

Printed in Great Britain
by Amazon